MW00533606

BOOK ANALYSIS

By Tom O'Brien

Slaughterhouse-Five
BY KURT VONNEGUT

Bright
≡Summaries.com

KURT VONNEGUT

AMERICAN NOVELIST AND SHORT STORY WRITER

- **Born in Indianapolis in 1922.**
- **Died in New York in 2007.**
- **Notable works:**
  - *Cat's Cradle* (1963), novel
  - *Jailbird* (1979), novel
  - *A Man Without a Country* (2005), essay collection

Kurt Vonnegut Jr. was born in Indianapolis, Indiana in 1992. His father Kurt Sr. was an architect, and his mother Edith was from a wealthy brewing family. Vonnegut wrote for and edited student newspapers at high school and Cornell University, where he found writing to be more enjoyable and less stressful than his degree in biochemistry.

Having enlisted in the US army in 1943, he was sent to Europe in late 1944, captured soon after, and lived through the Allied bombing of the German city of Dresden as a prisoner. When he returned home, he married Jane Marie Cox and studied anthropology at the University of Chicago, working as a reporter at night, before becoming a full-time writer in 1952. Vonnegut's early novels were extremely varied in style and content, sometimes containing elements of science fiction, and were moderately successful. He rose to fame when his 1969 novel *Slaughterhouse-Five* became a bestseller. He wrote sporadically for the next decade due to personal difficulties, but then published a series of successful novels through the 1980s and 90s. He died in 2007 in New York.

Today, Vonnegut's work remains extremely popular with the general public and is also widely studied in academic environments. Fellow writers often comment on the ease with which he wrote, despite the fragmented style he employed and the often difficult and painful subjects that he tackled.

SLAUGHTERHOUSE-FIVE

A SEMI-AUTOBIOGRAPHICAL ANTI-WAR NOVEL

- **Genre:** novel
- **Reference edition:** Vonnegut, K. (1991) *Slaughterhouse-Five*. New York: Dell Publishing.
- **1st edition:** 1969
- **Themes:** war, death, trauma, time, determinism

Between 13 and 15 February 1945, the British and US air forces bombarded the German city of Dresden with high-explosive bombs and incendiary devices, causing a firestorm that completely destroyed the centre of the city and killed approximately 25 000 people. A group of American prisoners of war survived in a meat storage bunker underground, among them a 22-year-old Kurt Vonnegut. For years after the war, Vonnegut struggled to write a book about Dresden, finally publishing the semi-autobiographical novel *Slaughterhouse-Five* in 1969. Following an opening chapter which deals with the author's troubles in writing the book, the novel tells the story of Billy Pilgrim, whose life shares many elements of Vonnegut's own wartime experience. Since Billy is subject to a kind of involuntary time travel, the narrative makes seemingly random jumps between the lead-up to and aftermath of the bombing and different parts of Billy's post-war life as a successful optometrist. Bizarrely, these episodes include Billy's abduction by aliens and his time spent on the planet Tralfamadore as an exhibit in a zoo. With its jumbled narrative and decidedly non-heroic protagonist, *Slaughterhouse-Five* portrays the senselessness of war from the perspective of the ordinary young people whose minds and lives are profoundly altered by it.

SUMMARY

A NOTE ON THE NOVEL'S STRUCTURE

Slaughterhouse-Five has a distinctly unconventional structure. The narrative takes the reader back and forth in time, and to a planet 446 120 000 000 000 000 miles away from Earth, as Billy Pilgrim involuntarily travels through time to different parts of his life. In this guide, the events of Billy Pilgrim's life are summarised in chronological order, after a brief summary of the novel's opening chapter, in which a narrator describes the challenges of writing a book about Dresden.

WRITING THE BOOK

A veteran of World War II spends the 1950s and 1960s attempting to write a novel about his experience as a prisoner of war in the German city of Dresden during the firebombing of the city by the British and American air forces. After several years spent studying anthropology, and working as a reporter and then a publicist, he eventually contacts Bernard V O'Hare, a friend from the war, and arranges a visit to discuss material for his book. Their discussion proves fruitless, but Bernard's wife Mary extracts a promise from the writer that he will not glamorise the war or the young soldiers who fought in it. After a tour of Eastern Europe with O'Hare, which includes a trip to Dresden, to conduct research for his book, the writer is finally able to complete the novel, whose protagonist will be called Billy Pilgrim.

BILLY PILGRIM'S CHILDHOOD

Billy Pilgrim is born in 1922 in Ilium, a town in New York State. He grows into a tall, awkward-looking youth, who is traumatised by his father's attempt to teach him how to swim by throwing him into the deep end of a pool, and by the graphic crucifix that his mother hangs on his bedroom wall. Aged 12, Billy visits the Grand Canyon in Arizona and Carlsbad Caverns in New Mexico with his mother and father. He is intensely frightened by the depth of the canyon and the darkness of the caves. Billy goes on to do reasonably well in high school.

BILLY PILGRIM IN WORLD WAR II AND ITS AFTERMATH

After enrolling in the Ilium School of Optometry, Billy's studies are cut short by the intervention of the United States in World War II. He enlists in the army and trains to become a chaplain's assistant, which includes very little combat training because his main duty will be playing the organ. He is sent to Europe in late 1944, shortly after his father is killed in a hunting accident. He fails to make contact with the chaplain he is supposed to be assisting due to an offensive by the German Army through Belgium and Luxembourg in what becomes known as the Battle of the Bulge.

Billy is stranded behind enemy lines with two scouts and a young soldier called Roland Weary, who is obsessed with the gruesome details of death, weapons and torture. Since Billy is untrained and underequipped, the scouts and Weary are frequently forced to rescue him from dangerous situations, and Billy displays a lack of interest in his own survival. Fed up with Billy and Weary's inexperience, the two scouts leave, and the two younger soldiers are soon captured and taken to a railway yard for transportation to a prison camp.

During the journey to the prison camp, many of the American prisoners, including Weary, die from exposure, exhaustion and infection. At the camp, the surviving prisoners are hosed off and given replacement clothes; Billy is given a ridiculous-looking fur coat in which he later finds a concealed diamond. He is threatened by a soldier called Paul Lazzaro, who blames Billy for Weary's death. The Americans are sent to join a group of British prisoners who welcome them warmly. During a theatrical performance by the British soldiers, Billy becomes hysterical and is given morphine. He is looked after by an older American called Edgar Derby.

After staying only one night at the camp, the Americans are transported to Dresden. Billy admires the beauty of the city, before the Americans are marched across the city and accommodated in a building named slaughterhouse-five. Here, their main job consists of cooking, packing and boxing malt syrup intended as a nutritional supplement for pregnant women.

After about a month, Dresden is attacked by Allied air forces and the American prisoners are taken to an underground meat locker. Only when they and their guards emerge do they realise the scale of the destruction: most buildings have been destroyed and the city is littered with rubble and corpses. After staying at an undamaged inn, the Americans are put to work removing bodies from the rubble of the destroyed city. A short time later, the Russian army advances through the city and frees the American captives.

When he returns home, Billy reenrols in the optometry school and proposes to the school's owner's daughter Valencia, before suffering a mental breakdown and being admitted to a veteran's hospital. There he meets Eliot Rosewater, who helps him to recover and introduces him to the work of Kilgore Trout, an unsuccessful science fiction writer. Billy marries Valencia, completes his training, and is given a lucrative role in her father's optometry firm.

BILLY PILGRIM'S LATER LIFE

Billy and Valencia have become rich, with a large house, a luxury car and shares in a hotel, but Billy is worried by his two habits of falling asleep at work and occasional fits of crying. He suffers a powerful psychological reaction when a barbershop quartet begins singing at his wedding anniversary celebrations, at which the writer Kilgore Trout is a guest.

Billy's son becomes an elite soldier and is fighting in Vietnam when Billy attends a club meeting where one of the members makes a speech in favour of carpet bombing North Vietnam. Despite his first-hand experience of a bombing raid against civilian targets 20 years earlier, Billy remains unaffected by the speech.

After his daughter's wedding reception in 1967, Billy is apparently abducted by aliens and taken to the planet Tralfamadore, where the Tralfamadorians, a race of single-eyed aliens shaped like toilet plungers, confine him to a zoo for observation. They bring him an actress named Montana Wildhack as a companion, and she and Billy live together as a couple for some time, even having a child together. The Tralfamadorians explain their view of time and philosophy of life to Billy, who is seduced and comforted by the belief that events are predetermined and cannot be changed by a single person's actions, and that trauma and death can be ignored by focusing on the happy and carefree parts of life.

Billy is apparently returned to Earth at the same moment that he left it. Later, on the way to an optometry conference, Billy's plane crashes and he is the only survivor. While she is driving to the hospital to see him, Valencia crashes her car. She continues driving, but the faulty exhaust pumps carbon monoxide into the car's interior, eventually killing her. When Billy recovers, he decides that he wants to tell the world about his abduction and promote the merits of Tralfamadorian philosophy. He travels to New York City, where he manages to get onto a live radio show. As he starts telling his story, he is kicked out of the studio. A visit to a bookstore raises doubts about the reality of his Tralfamadore experience, before his daughter comes to the City to pick him up. Billy makes a tape which predicts his death by laser-gun in 1976 at the hands of Paul Lazzaro, who threatened Billy back in 1945. The tape also predicts that Billy will have gained a significant following for Tralfamadorian philosophy, and China will have attacked the United States with nuclear weapons. He is at peace with the idea of his of his own death.

CHARACTER STUDY

THE NARRATOR

The unnamed narrator of the novel's first and final chapters is a writer and former soldier who struggles to produce a book about the bombing of Dresden, and who describes himself as "on old fart with his memories and his Pall Malls [cigarettes]" (p. 7). So many of the details about the narrator overlap with Vonnegut's real life that we can assume the first chapter is almost completely autobiographical. These details include:

- A trip to Eastern Europe (including Dresden) funded by the Guggenheim Foundation.
- Time spent working as a night reporter in Chicago.
- Time spent working as a publicist for the General Electric Corporation in Schenectady, New York.
- A daughter called Nanny (Nannette).
- A heavy smoking habit.

The narrator also inserts himself into Billy Pilgrim's story several times:

- After Billy is captured by the German army and the soldiers are being sorted according to rank, the narrator says that he and his friend Bernard V. O'Hare were present as fellow prisoners.
- Just before Billy is supposedly abducted by the Tralfamadorians, he receives a phone call from a drunk and "could almost smell his breath—mustard gas and roses" (p. 73), implying that it is the narrator on the other end of the line.
- When Billy visits the latrine at the POW camp the Americans share briefly with British soldiers, one of those suffering the effects of food poisoning is the narrator.
- When Billy Pilgrim and the other prisoners are put to work removing corpses from the rubble of Dresden, the narrator says that he and Bernard O'Hare were also present.

The opening chapter's commentary on the author's writing process, and the self-insertion of the author/narrator within the story are both common metafictional techniques (techniques that draw attention to the 'constructedness', or existence as fiction, of a story). Adding the metafictional character of the narrator serves a double purpose. First, the opening chapter serves as justification for the jumbled narrative and lack of common storytelling techniques—"climaxes and thrills and characterization and wonderful dialogue and suspense and confrontations" (p. 5), as the narrator himself puts it. Second, the narrator's appearances lend authenticity to the war sections of Billy Pilgrim's narrative, distinguishing them from the pure fiction of Billy's later life and his alien abduction. It seems as if Vonnegut wanted to protect himself against potential accusations of poor storytelling, a failure to treat war with the seriousness it deserves, or an unflattering portrayal of American soldiers.

BILLY PILGRIM

Like Vonnegut himself, Billy Pilgrim was born in 1922 and survived the firebombing of Dresden as a 22-year-old prisoner in the slaughterhouse of the novel's title. He is described as "funny looking youth—tall and weak, and shaped like a bottle of Coca-Cola" (p. 23) He is (supposedly) distinguished from the rest of humanity by his involuntary trips through time to different portions of his life.

The author presents Billy as being as far from the archetypal courageous 'war hero' as possible. He is terrified by childhood trips to the Grand Canyon and Carlsbad Caverns (a cave system) in New Mexico, and does not seem to have grown out of this fearfulness by the time he is sent to fight in Europe. He is both a naturally incompetent soldier and the victim of a lack of training and equipment. He shows almost no initiative at any point of the story, allowing circumstances and other people to dictate his own actions, both during the war and his professional life. This only changes after the plane crash and the death of his wife Veronica, when Billy begins to become a kind of evangelist for Tralfamadorian philosophy.

He is treated with varying levels of contempt by many of the other characters in the novel, beginning with his father, who throws him into a deep pool to force him to learn to swim. This is followed by bullying at the hands of the other young soldiers Roland Weary and Paul Lazzaro, and the other prisoners in the train carriage on the way to the prisoner camp. In later episodes, the military historian Captain Rumfoord develops an irrational hatred of Billy when they are recovering in the same hospital after Billy's plane accident, and Billy's own daughter Barbara shows little sympathy for his odd behaviour after his recovery. Exceptions to the general contempt in which Billy is held are his wife Veronica, who is extremely devoted to Billy, and Eliot Rosewater, a fellow hospital patient who helps Billy to recover from a breakdown.

Because Billy Pilgrim shares certain parts of Vonnegut's own personal history, it is worth investigating some of Billy's character traits and experiences that diverge from Vonnegut's own. The first of these is Billy's apparently unquestioning religious faith, which "most soldiers found putrid" (p. 31), and his wartime role as a chaplain's assistant (Vonnegut himself was trained as a scout). Vonnegut perhaps means for Billy's blind faith to account for his general passivity, later leading to his wholehearted acceptance of the Tralfamadorian worldview and his inability to cope with the reality of his war experience.

A second divergence is Billy's choice of profession. Billy's career as an optometrist could be seen as simply another aspect of his passive nature and lack of initiative: his home town of Ilium, Ohio is home to the optometry school where Billy trains and a large existing market for optometry services and products. However, after Billy's supposed abduction to Tralfamadore, his choice of profession takes on added meaning. In his attempts to popularise Tralfamadorian philosophy, Billy believes that he is "prescribing corrective lenses for Earthling souls" (p. 29). If we accept that Tralfamadore is a delusion or coping mechanism, as is suggested by later events, than it can be argued that Billy's profession and his semi-religious view of it are used by Vonnegut to gently satirise religious figures who believe that their message would provide salvation if only enough people would listen to it.

THE TRALFAMADORIANS

The Tralfamadorians are an alien race who, according to Billy, kidnap him and display him in a zoo on their planet Tralfalmadore, bringing him the actress Montana Wildhack as a companion. They resemble toilet plungers with a hand on the top of the handle and a single eye in the palm of the hand, and they can "see in four dimensions" (p. 26). Billy explains this by saying that "the Tralfamadorians can look at all the different moments just the way we can look at a stretch of the Rocky Mountains" (p. 27). Because of this supposed ability, they claim that all moments are fixed and – from the human perspective – predetermined, and pity humans for their inability to see in this way. Their 'novels' are "brief clumps of symbols" (p. 88), designed to be 'read' simultaneously, with "no beginning, no middle, no end, no morals, no suspense, no causes no effects." (*ibid.*) When Billy asks them whether they feel threatened by the destructiveness of Earth's human civilisation they dismiss his concerns, telling him that "we have wars as horrible as any you have ever seen" (p. 117), and claim to know that the universe will be destroyed by one of their own experiments. Billy is seduced by their philosophy before returning to Earth.

Although Billy's descriptions of and interactions with the Tralfamadorians are described as matter-of-factly as the rest of Billy's story, their existence is called into question later when Billy visits a seedy bookstore and finds a novel by Kilgore Trout that has a plot similar to Billy's abduction, and a magazine article speculating on the whereabouts of Montana Wildhack. This suggests that Billy's supposed abduction was a delusion and perhaps an elaborate coping mechanism that allows Billy to deal with his Dresden experience by adopting the imaginary Tralfamadorian view that traumatic events are predestined, and can (and should) be filtered out of an intelligent being's experience of life.

BILLY PILGRIM'S FAMILY

Since the novel focuses so heavily on Billy Pilgrim himself, other characters are not nearly as developed, and we only find out about them as they relate to his life and preoccupations. The members of his family include:

- **Billy's wife Valencia**: Valencia is the overweight daughter of the owner of the school of optometry where Billy studies. While she is devoted to Billy, Billy is indifferent to her, even describing his marriage proposal as a "symptom of his disease" (p. 107). Her character is used as further evidence of Billy's passivity and indifference, and he shows little reaction to her accidental death, apparently more concerned about spreading Tralfamadorian philosophy.

- **Billy's daughter Barbara**: Barbara is "a fairly pretty girl, except that she had legs like an Edwardian grand piano" (p. 29). She argues with Billy when he attempts to spread the story of his abduction after the plane crash and Valencia's death, suggesting that Tralfamadore is a figment of Billy's imagination, and believes him to have suffered brain damage in the crash. Barbara perhaps represents the difficulties faced by people living with those affected by the trauma of war.

- **Billy's son Robert:** Robert goes through a period of delinquency before reforming and becoming an elite soldier in the Vietnam War. His only direct appearance in the narrative occurs during His parents' wedding anniversary celebrations. Billy seems unable to communicate with his son, who is yet to become a soldier at this point. This brief meeting perhaps represents the missed opportunity of older veterans to communicate the trauma of war to younger people, who consequently enter later conflicts under the influence of ideas of

patriotism, duty and adventure rather than
with a true sense of what war entails.

BILLY PILGRIM'S FELLOW SOLDIERS

- **Roland Weary**: Weary is an 18-year-old soldier
  who accompanies Billy as they search for a
  way out of Luxembourg after the Battle of
  the Bulge. He is "stupid, fat and mean, and
  smelled like bacon no matter how much he
  washed" (p. 35). He has an active fantasy life in
  which he is always cast as a hero, a leader and
  popular with his fellow soldiers, whereas the
  reality is that he is not much more competent
  than Billy and is disliked by the two unnamed
  scouts who travel with them. He has an un-
  healthy obsession with weapons and torture,
  and eventually physically assaults Billy in a fit
  of anger. The character is perhaps intended as
  an antidote to the heroism and selflessness of
  soldiers in contemporary fictional portrayals
  of war.

- **Paul Lazzaro**: Paul Lazzaro is another young
  soldier who, under the influence of a dying
  Roland Weary's description of Billy's incompe-
  tence and stupidity, develops a hatred of Billy
  and vows to avenge Weary's death after the

war. It is implied that he will be successful in this mission when Billy makes a tape recording after his plane crash and trip to New York City, in which he predicts his own death at the hands of Lazzaro in 1976. Even more than Weary, the character of Lazzaro fulfils the narrator's promise to Mary O'Hare not to glamorise the American soldiers who fought in World War II.

- **Edgar Derby**: Derby is an older soldier who displays almost the opposite characteristics to Weary and Lazzaro. He has a pleasant nature, is kind to Billy, and shows strong leadership capabilities, but is summarily executed for looting a teapot in the aftermath of the Dresden bombing. Derby's death is perhaps the clearest single representation of the tragedy and senselessness of war in *Slaughterhouse-Five*, because of the impossibility (acknowledged by Vonnegut) of accurately portraying the many thousands of deaths caused by the bombing. The narrator's assertion that "one guy I know really *was* shot in Dresden for taking a teapot that wasn't his" (p. 1) gives an added weight to Derby's death beyond that of a purely fictional character.

ELLIOT ROSEWATER

Elliot Rosewater, who also features in several other novels by Vonnegut, is fellow patient of Billy's in the veteran's hospital after Billy suffers a mental breakdown shortly after returning from the war. He is friendly to Billy and introduces him to the novels of Kilgore Trout, which Billy reads avidly. Elliot's treatment of Billy reflects the advice often given to people who live with sufferers of depression: that they should engage with the person, remain non-judgemental of the person's depressive attitude and behaviour, and offer practical ways for the person to 'come to themselves'. Vonnegut himself suffered from depression and would undoubtedly have experienced both constructive and unconstructive interactions with friends and family members. Although he helps Billy, Rosewater may have also indirectly provided him with the basis for his Tralfamadore delusion.

KILGORE TROUT

Kilgore Trout, like Eliot Rosewater, features in other novels by Vonnegut as well as

Slaughterhouse-Five. He is an unsuccessful science-fiction author, whose only two fans are Billy and Eliot Rosewater. Along with the narrator and Billy himself, Trout is the only character to suspect Billy's time-travelling ability, and one of his novels gives Billy the inspiration for his Tralfamadore delusion. Kilgore Trout is intended as a satirical nod to the lack of respect accorded to science fiction by the literary establishment, which Vonnegut was critical of.

ANALYSIS

AN ANTI-WAR NOVEL

When *Slaughterhouse-Five* was published in 1969, it soon became immensely popular with students and others who opposed the ongoing war in Vietnam. Vonnegut was invited to speak at many different colleges around the US and at political rallies. That the novel expresses the horror, destructiveness and the senselessness of both the firebombing of Dresden and war in general – and its effects on survivors – cannot be doubted. On the very first page, the narrator remarks of the modern, partially rebuilt Dresden that "there must be tons of human bone meal in the ground" (p. 1), and at the close of the novel Billy Pilgrim is forced to work in "corpse mines" (p. 214) of Dresden to extract bodies from the rubble. Many other disturbing events are depicted in the intervening pages of the novel. But it is worth analysing whether the novel stops at being a mere depiction of war and its effects, or whether it can be read as a pacifist call to actively oppose war.

The character of Billy Pilgrim is passive by nature and seems to agree when Captain Rumfoord, a military historian, tries to justify the bombing of Dresden as he and Billy recover in hospital afte

r Billy's plane crash (p. 198), and also "was not moved to protest the bombing of North Vietnam" (p. 60). Moreover, he accepts the Tralfamadorian conception of time in which all events, including wars, already exist along the 'fourth dimension' and can cannot be averted by the will of individuals. In fact, he travels straight from the hospital room he shares with Rumfoord to New York in attempt to promote the deterministic views of the Tralfamadorians on the radio and television. Billy Pilgrim therefore sees no point in anti-war activism and hopes that others will come to share his views.

In contrast to this, by framing Billy's narrative with opening and closing chapters told by an almost completely autobiographical narrator, Vonnegut imbues the novel as a whole with a more actively anti-war slant. At first, the narrator seems to share Billy's beliefs, when he agrees with the director Harrison Star's feeling that wars are "as easy to stop as glaciers" (p. 3). However, at other points in the chapter the narrator's actions can be seen as small-scale but active opposition to war,. When he visits his friend Bernard O'Hare, the narrator cannot work out why Mary O'Hare is angry with him until she confronts him with the accusation that he will glamorise the war in his forthcoming book, saying "you'll be played in the movies by Frank Sinatra and John Wayne or some of those other glamorous, war-loving, dirty old men" (p. 14). When the narrator assures Mary that his book will contain the truth about the war being mainly fought by inexperienced young men (or "babies like the ones upstairs" [*ibid.*], as Mary puts it), they become friends. Elsewhere in the chapter, the narrator tells us that he has forbidden his sons to be involved in future massacres or to have anything to do with producing the machinery of war, in contrast to Billy's son, who grows up to be a soldier.

Vonnegut seems to present Billy's attitude towards war as an understandable, but still mis-guided reaction to his experiences, while the nar-rator – wiser and more capable of self-reflection than Billy – conveys Vonnegut's true thoughts about war; that it *is* inevitable, but that good people can, at the least, find ways not to be party to the destruction, and question the intentions of those who advocate or glorify it.

SO IT GOES

On more than 100 occasions throughout the novel, Vonnegut follows instances of death with the refrain 'so it goes'. This ranges from the literal deaths of 130 000 people (though historians have placed the official figure closer to 25 000 in the bombing of Dresden (p. 177), to the 'death' of a bottle of champagne left open for too long after Billy Pilgrim's daughter's wedding reception (p. 73). The meaning of the phrase is something similar to 'that's life' or 'shit happens'; if we don't believe in a 'higher power' (Vonnegut was an atheist and humanist), then death is not simply inevitable, but also without higher meaning. This fits with – or perhaps even originates from – the deterministic philosophy of the Tralfamadorians, who view all events, including death, as predestined and unchangeable.

The refrain is used both by the narrator in the opening chapter and then throughout Billy Pilgrim's narrative, so one possible reading is

that Billy and the narrator share the same misin-
terpretation of Tralfamadorian philosophy and
accept that nothing can be done about tragic
events in the past, present or future. However,
another possible interpretation is that the phrase
is only used because, in the words of the narrator
in the first chapter, "there is nothing intelligent
to say about a massacre" (p. 19). In this reading,
the phrase 'so it goes' does not signify passive
acceptance, but contains all the rage, grief and
guilt felt by people who experience tragic events
and survive, but are unable to express those
feelings in any meaningful way. The ironic use of
the phrase for the 'death' of trivial objects can be
seen as a kind of dark humour that accentuates,
rather than trivialises, the horror of actual death.

POST-TRAUMATIC STRESS DISORDER

There are several episodes in the novel in which
Billy Pilgrim clearly shows signs of mental
disturbance. There are three major instances
of this that interfere with his surprisingly
successful post-war life. The first is the "mild
nervous collapse" (p. 24) he suffers shortly after

returning from the war, which leads to his stay in the veteran's hospital, shock treatments and his meeting with Elliot Rosewater. The second is his abduction to the zoo on Tralfamadore (if we share Billy's daughter's very reasonable view that this is a powerful delusion). The third is Billy's belief that he is "spastic in time" (p. 23), which accounts for the disordered narrative of the novel. There are also less severe disturbances, such as Billy's habit of quietly crying to himself, and a powerful but transitory episode in which he reacts strongly to the barbershop quartet at his and Valencia's 18th wedding anniversary.

The episode at the anniversary is particularly interesting because it describes the kind of crisis often experienced by people with Post Traumatic Stress Disorder (PTSD). For people with PTSD, specific sensory experiences in the present can often trigger recollections of a traumatic event that occurred in the past. The experience is often far more vivid than anything they can access with their 'normal' memory, and may be accompanied by physical symptoms like sweating or breathing difficulties. In some cases, the pain of the original trauma is so powerful that sufferers only experience these physical symptoms when triggered, having repressed the associated memory entirely. At the party, Billy suffers a strong mental and physical reaction to the singing of a barbershop quartet, which causes other guests to think he is having a heart attack. He then thinks to himself: "Here was proof that he had a great big secret somewhere inside, and he could not imagine what it was" (p. 173). Afterwards, he links the crisis to the memory of the faces of the German guards as they led the American prisoners out of the slaughterhouse after the firebombing, and seeing "little logs lying around" (p. 179) which were in fact the corpses of people killed by the firestorm.

In a much less pronounced way than Billy, the narrator also describes symptoms in himself that might be signs of PTSD. He mentions that "I have this disease late at night sometimes, involving alcohol and the telephone" (p. 4), and when he and his friend Bernard O'Hare are trying to recall their Dresden experience, they are only able to produce one inconsequential story each (p. 14). Neither of them is able to recall anything about the bombing, which is often a sign of PTSD. This is further illustrated by the long and painful writing process experienced by the narrator. That Vonnegut was able to reproduce the effects of trauma so strikingly in his character Billy Pilgrim, before PTSD was a widely-recognised phenomenon, indicates that Vonnegut himself perhaps suffered from PTSD and recognised the same kind of behaviours and symptoms in other veterans he knew.

Treatment for PTSD often involves confronting the traumatic memory repeatedly until it loses its power over the mind and body. For Vonnegut, *Slaughterhouse-Five* was the product of a partly successful treatment, a therapeutic process, and marked the beginning of a more successful career. His character Billy, who suffers the additional trauma of the plane crash, and lacks Vonnegut's ability to express himself, goes on to develop the delusion of Tralfamadore as a kind of protection against his traumatic memories, leaving him unable to live a normal life. Billy's post-war life illustrates the dangers of leaving supressed traumas untreated.

FURTHER REFLECTION

SOME QUESTIONS TO THINK ABOUT...

- What effect does the lack of a 'traditional' narrative structure in *Slaughterhouse-Five* have on you as a reader?
- Why do you think Vonnegut included elements of science fiction in a semi-autobiographical novel about World War II?
- Why do you think Kurt Vonnegut included the opening chapter about the writing of the book?
- What do you think is the significance of the birdcall "poo-tee-weet" (p. 215) that Billy Pilgrim notices after the bombing of Dresden?
- Why does Billy keep a copy of the serenity prayer used by members of Alcoholics Anonymous on the wall of his office? Do you think Vonnegut approves of the prayer?
- *Slaughterhouse-Five* has often been banned by school districts and individual schools in the United States. Why do you think this is?

- In the opening chapter, the narrator mentions various real-life books and authors in a positive light, including Louis-Ferdinand Céline (1894-1961), a French novelist notorious for a series of rabidly anti-Semitic pamphlets. This, along with the single, brief mention of Nazi atrocities against Jews in the novel, led to accusations that Vonnegut intentionally ignored this subject in his work. Do you think these accusations have any validity? Why? Why not?
- The analysis shows the contrast between Vonnegut successfully confronting the trauma of Dresden and Billy failing to do. Do you think it is essential for both individuals and societies as a whole to confront past traumatic events? Why? Why not?

We want to hear from you!
Leave a comment on your online library
and share your favourite books on social media!

FURTHER READING

REFERENCE EDITION

- Vonnegut, K. (1991) *Slaughterhouse-Five*. New York: Dell Publishing.

REFERENCE STUDIES

- Vanderwerken, D. L. (2013) Kurt Vonnegut's *Slaughterhouse-Five* at Forty: Billy Pilgrim—Even More a Man of Our Times. *Critique: Studies in Contemporary Fiction.* 54(1), pp. 46-55.
- Vees-Gulani, S. (2003) Diagnosing Billy Pilgrim: A Psychiatric Approach to Kurt Vonnegut's *Slaughterhouse-Five*. *Critique: Studies in Contemporary Fiction.* 44(2), pp. 175-184.

ADDITIONAL SOURCES

- Marvin, T. F. (2002). *Kurt Vonnegut: A Critical Companion.* Westport Ct: Greenwood Publishing Group.
- Shields, C. J. (2011) *And So It Goes: Kurt Vonnegut, A Life.* New York: Henry Holt.

ADAPTATIONS

- *Slaughterhouse-Five.* (1972) [Film]. George Roy Hill. Dir. USA: Vanadas Productions, Universal Pictures.

Although the editor makes every effort to
verify the accuracy of the information published,
BrightSummaries.com accepts no responsibility for
the content of this book.

www.brightsummaries.com

Ebook EAN: 9782808013208

Paperback EAN: 9782808013215

Legal Deposit: D/2018/12603/418

Cover: © Primento

Digital conception by Primento, the digital partner of
publishers.

Made in the USA
Columbia, SC
31 January 2022

55096783R00033